Everyday
Scriptures

Everyday Scriptures

Our Story *in* God's Story

Lois Spear, OP

Saint Mary's Press
Christian Brothers Publications
Winona, Minnesota

In memory of Mary Tardiff, OP,
a woman of courage

Genuine recycled paper with 10% post-consumer waste.
Printed with soy-based ink.

The publishing team included Carl Koch, development editor; Rebecca
Fairbank, manuscript editor; Hollace Storkel, typesetter; Maurine R. Twait,
art director; Cindi Ramm, cover designer; Vicki Shuck, illustrator; pre-
press, printing, and binding by the graphics division of Saint Mary's Press.

The psalms in this book are from *Psalms Anew: In Inclusive Language*,
compiled by Nancy Schreck and Maureen Leach (Winona, MN: Saint
Mary's Press, 1986). Copyright © 1986 by Saint Mary's Press. All rights
reserved.

   All other scriptural quotations in this book are from the New Revised
Standard Version of the Bible. Copyright © 1989 by the Division of Chris-
tian Education of the National Council of the Churches of Christ in the
United States of America. All rights reserved.

   The poem "Abou Ben Adhem," by Leigh Hunt on pages 61–62 is
quoted from *Poems That Every Child Should Know: A Selection of the Best
Poems of All Times for Young People*, edited by Mary E. Burt (New York:
Grosset and Dunlap, 1904), pages 88, 88, and 89, respectively. Copyright
© 1904 by Doubleday, Page and Company.

Printed in the United States of America

Printing: 9 8 7 6 5 4 3 2 1

Year: 2007 06 05 04 03 02 01 00 99

ISBN 0-88489-549-1

Contents

Preface

Everyone likes a good story. Stories engage the listener, stimulate the imagination, and suggest another level of understanding. No wonder Jesus spoke in parables. The meditations in this book are an invitation, through storytelling, to connect the Scriptures with our daily life.

We don't know who told the first stories. We can imagine prehistoric humans gathered around campfires, perhaps telling the first stories in sign language, with grunts and howls to punctuate the narration. Over time these sounds became symbols, words rich in meaning. We don't have to look far for examples of this kind of storytelling. Long before Europeans appeared on American shores, Native Americans used stories to keep alive the memory, values, and rituals of their tribe and to pass them on to later generations.

The Bible, a book of books, contains the recorded stories told and retold by the Jewish people. It is not a history, yet it contains the great truths of our creation, broad-stroked to show how our common ancestors viewed the universe.

As Christians we believe that the Bible is divinely inspired, though it must be read with an understanding of myth, and with attention to the historical epoch in which it was transcribed. The Hebrew Scriptures (Old Testament) have value both on their own terms and as a foundation for the Christian Testament (New Testament). In the Christian Testament, however, passages hurling imprecations at enemies or vowing "an eye for an eye" kind of justice have been replaced by the commandment to love God and neighbor. The psalmist's prayer for destruction of enemies, "Slay them, . . . / Destroy them in your anger" (59:11–13), is not condoned by Jesus, though it can still be found in the hearts of Christians.

Bible illiteracy was understandable in the medieval ages when most people couldn't read. Statues and miracle, or mystery, plays filled the gap. With the invention of the printing press, the Bible came within reach of a mass audience.

Luther and other reformers urged all Christians to study and pray the Bible. For Catholics, however, the hierarchy's concern that the Scriptures might be misinterpreted led them to discourage Bible reading unless under clerical guidance— at Mass or in religious formation programs.

From hindsight we can see merit in the concern about misreading the Scriptures. Fundamentalists often read the Bible as a literal, historical account. Others read passages from the Bible to document the latest fads. Bible illiteracy persists into the twenty-first century.

Some believers have never been encouraged to make the Bible part of the ordinary events of their day. However, the transcendent God of high heaven is also the immanent God dwelling in human hearts and in all creation. Jesus, redeemer God, walks among us in perfect unity with the creator God and the sanctifier God.

When we reflect on our own stories, no matter how lowly they seem, we trace God's footsteps in our life. We stand in awe of a God who loves us and wills to walk with us through the light and shadows of the day.

Communal prayer can add a further dimension to our reflections. Jesus said, "Where two or three are gathered in my name, I am there among them" (Matthew 18:20). Our stories, combined with those of all creation, play out with God in the midst of people gathered in faith.

Unfortunately, opportunities for communal prayer are limited unless we actively search out Bible study classes and small Christian communities, or organize a prayer group on our own. Also, we have learned to refrain from telling our stories through fear of being ridiculed. Note, for example, the response at meetings when we are asked to introduce ourselves. We squirm and then offer banalities such as where we live, our occupation, our favorite sports. Missing from the introduction is anything personal: our feelings, hopes, disappointments.

The meditations in this book seek to entice you to greater depth in your personal prayer and to a commitment to communal prayer wherever it may be found: in your church, home, or neighborhood. The meditations link the countless stories in our own life with stories in the Scriptures. We laugh with Sarah when she learns she will have a child in her old age (Genesis 18:12–15), mourn with Rachel over the loss of her children (Matthew 2:18), and rejoice with the father when the prodigal son returns (Luke 15:11–32). We have similar experiences to share.

Each meditation has four parts: story, Scripture, reflection, and prayer. My story and the Scripture story set the stage for the reflections. The reflections are intended to stir your personal meditation, prayer, and, if you pray with a group, shared prayer and reflection. All the meditations conclude with prayer: meditative, vocal, or a suggestion for action.

If you are praying alone, I urge you to designate a certain amount of time for meditation as part of your daily schedule. A designated prayer time and a familiar prayer space will help encourage a quiet conversation with God.

Across the centuries Jesus and the prophets speak to us through story and parable. When we respond with our own stories, we reflect the great story of Emmanuel, God-with-us. May this book of meditations lead you into a closer union with the God whose story unfurls in the Scriptures and in our own life.

Lois Spear, OP

PART I

Gifts

gift. A notable capacity or talent; something voluntarily transferred by one person to another without compensation

Everything Is Gift

When I was growing up, everything depended on the farm. In good years, when there was plenty of rain and a long growing season, our crops flourished, and we had corn, wheat, and beans to store or sell. On the other hand, a farm disaster, like hail, grasshoppers, or corn borers, could bring us to the edge of bankruptcy.

One hot July afternoon when we could almost hear the corn growing, a violent thunderstorm erupted from the west. The warning signals were few: an unnatural stillness in the air, a certain uneasiness among the livestock. Then the storm broke. Everyone raced for cover. Most of us ran to the house where, with my mother, we stood at the kitchen window and watched the trees quake in the wind and anything loose fly past us as the storm vented its fury.

Then it came, soft at first, but growing in an increasing staccato: hailstones as big as golf balls. No corn crop could withstand this battering. The long narrow fronds and delicate early ears would be shredded to bits.

My mother, in a characteristic gesture, flung her apron over her head and cried. How could this catastrophe have happened? She regularly blessed our house and farm with holy water, hung crucifixes in every room, and gathered the family for evening prayer. Yet God still had not protected us.

After a few minutes, the tears stopped. Mother dropped her apron and told us kids to grab pails and go outside. The storm was over now. No use crying over spilled milk. We rushed into the yard and began picking up the hail. With no electricity in our farm home, ice was a rarity in July. One of us pulled out our old, hand-cranked ice-cream maker. Mother made a delicious custard, and the whole family enjoyed a homemade ice-cream treat.

Pause. Reflect on God's many gifts to you, especially those you least appreciated at the time.

Scripture

Read the story of Elijah and the widow, 1 Kings 17:7–16.

Reflection

Everyone faces adversity. Sometimes it's a minor setback: a car that won't start, a persistent head cold, an unkind remark by a coworker. Major setbacks are harder to comprehend: loss of a season's crop, sudden unemployment, a heart attack, the death of a family member or friend. We can spend the rest of our days mourning these losses or, like my mother, choose in time to accept everything as gift. The old adage, "It's an ill wind that blows nobody good," applies only when we refuse to search through a setback, seeking the positive side, the personal growth it can engender.

In the Scripture story, the widow and her son, like our farm family, suffered from weather-related setbacks: a violent storm, a long drought. Even though she and her son were facing starvation, the widow reached out to someone in need. She saw an opportunity to help, and she responded immediately. A gift given in the name of God will always be given back somehow, and so as Elijah tells the widow and Jesus tells us after the Resurrection, "Do not be afraid."

Can you think of a similar experience of sudden loss in your life? If so, recall the experience in some detail. How did it help you to grow? If you had to relive the experience, would you change things? Why or why not?

Prayer. Think of two strong women—one from the Scriptures and the other from your own life. Reflect on these women's lives as gifts. Then ask God for the grace to live each day in the realization that everything, even adversity, is gift.

On Using Our Gifts

Long before large families became unpopular, my brother Bill and his wife raised nine kids on their Iowa farm. The older kids looked after the little ones, spending hours together in chores and play. Baby-sitters weren't needed in the home, and the grown-ups never complained about kids underfoot. Tom, the oldest son, was the ringleader among the siblings. He could conjure up endless sources of entertainment—from riding Betsy the cow to sailing high over the trees in the old tire swing in the yard.

Bill liked to attend farm auctions, often coming home with antiques of dubious value. They rusted outside, giving the farmyard a dilapidated look. One of Bill's happier purchases—a small, very battered organ—became a challenge to Tom's talent and ingenuity. The bellows had rotted, making it impossible to pump air into the organ. Without air, the organ wouldn't play when the footpedals were pushed.

Among the junk in the farm's toolshed, Tom discovered an old vacuum cleaner, discarded after his mother had bought a new one. Tom attached the vacuum cleaner to the opening where the bellows entered the organ. When the vacuum cleaner was plugged in and the footpedals were pushed vigorously, the organ would play. The tone was squeaky and off pitch, but what did that matter to a bunch of kids?

Another challenge: The vacuum cleaner was noisy, threatening to drown out the organ. No problem. Although Tom could not read notes, he knew by heart the melody for "Amazing Grace." He rounded up his siblings and taught them the hymn. Then, as the organ wheezed, they sang gustily, blotting out the roar of the vacuum cleaner.

As he grew older, Tom used his gifts well. He's now a successful businessman who uses his musical ability as choir director in his parish church.

Pause. Reflect for a moment on a special gift you possess and the time when you first became aware of it.

Scripture

Read about the gifts of the Spirit, 1 Corinthians 12:4–11.

Reflection

The Holy Spirit embraces all creation, breathing gifts of love into human hearts. Each gift is priceless—from the mighty prophecies of Isaiah to the generosity of spirit displayed by the widow as she dropped her mite into the temple treasury (Mark 12:41–44). Our gifts are equally valuable.

We can use our gifts for ourselves and others, or we can let them atrophy and die. By using his musical ability, Tom also nourished spiritual gifts: bonding among family members, a sense of awe at God's amazing grace, and a commitment to use gifts and talents in the liturgical prayer of the church.

Think about some of the members of your family or local community. Name a gift you associate with each individual. Then decide what your greatest gift is. The next time you gather with your family or community, take time to recognize each person's gifts, including your own.

Prayer.

God of wisdom, help me to discover the gifts you have given me.

God of humility, help me to accept your gifts with love and gratitude.

God of love, help me to use my gifts for my own good and the good of others.

A Gift Refused

Gifts are a timeless way of celebrating significant mileposts in our life. The giver also receives. For instance, she or he receives feelings of being accepted and of serving others. But when does the balance between giver and receiver become disrupted, the receiver feeling victimized and used as a foil to demonstrate the giver's superiority and magnanimity?

The question arose when I lived with Kaye in a small community in Salt Lake City. The dynamics were all wrong. We lived, worked, and prayed together, yet we remained strangers. Conflicts were never met with a healthy burst of anger that might have cleared the air.

During one summer some friends visited me, and we decided to explore Heber City, site of a small scenic railroad called the Heber Creeper. After the ride we visited a craft shop where I bought a vase for Kaye. My motives weren't clear at the time. Was this a sincere peace token, or was it a way to demonstrate my bigheartedness in overlooking another's perceived faults?

In any case, Kaye accepted the gift in a stiff and pained manner that spoke volumes about her feelings. A few days later, the vase appeared among the other house items in our pantry. The gift had been refused. I felt hurt and humiliated. With time the hurt ebbed away, but I still have that vase, a reminder that true gifts proceed from a simple and open heart.

Pause. Consider a recent gift you gave to a friend or loved one. Try to clarify your motives.

Scripture

Read the story of the rich young man, Mark 10:17–22.

Reflection

It's socially acceptable to offer gifts on important occasions like birthdays or bridal showers. Gifts from casual acquaintances don't usually have the power to move us deeply. We accept them with smiles and words of gratitude, sometimes wondering to ourselves how we'll ever dispose of them. It's the gifts from loved ones that matter most. These gifts can enchant us and fill us with feelings of love and support. Sadly, the opposite may also be true. We long to reject gifts from people we dislike, but kindness or social inhibitions keep us from offending the giver.

Unlike my gift to Kaye, Jesus' gift to the rich young man sprang from no conflicting motives. Jesus offered eternal life. The young man sadly refused, unable to discard his possessions at that point in his life.

Recall a time when you felt the presence of God through a spiritual gift, accompanied perhaps by a sense of peace, joy, or pain. Did you accept the gift? How did it alter your life?

What pure-hearted gifts can you offer to those you love? Consider a handmade item such as a loaf of bread, or an act of service such as an evening of baby-sitting.

Prayer. Jesus, through your death and Resurrection, you gifted us with life, faith, and the hope of salvation. Help us to appreciate your generosity by sharing with others simple gifts from the heart.

Unexpected Gifts

Persistence pays off. If you really want something and are persistent, chances are you'll get it. Sister Agatha was like that. She took pride in being principal chance saleswoman for Viterbo College's annual fund-raiser. The tickets were expensive, but the list of prizes was awesome: every conceivable kind of gift or service that volunteers could wrangle from city merchants.

When Agatha entered my office one bright morning, I reached for my purse, knowing that my visitor wouldn't leave until I had purchased at least one ticket. As I handed over the cash, I explained that this was a total donation. I'd never won anything at raffles or games of chance. My luck wasn't erratic; it was nonexistent. "Business will take me out of state on the night of the raffle," I explained to Agatha, and asked her to keep the ticket stub for me. This business of being out of state at raffle time, I mused after she left, might work to my advantage. Maybe it would break my losing streak.

When I returned to the office after my trip, Agatha was one of the first to greet me. "You won something," she said. "Let me get it." She returned in a few minutes with a boom box a yard long. It had every contraption to cheer a teenage heart: tape player, recorder, AM radio, batteries, electric cord, and lots of high-volume capability!

I thanked Agatha for the gift and, with no little amusement, agreed that my luck had finally changed. Not really needing the boom box, I discretely returned it to the college.

Pause. Consider the circumstances surrounding an unexpected gift you've received.

Scripture

Read about the importunate friend, Luke 11:5–8.

Reflection

Persistent efforts may result in unexpected gifts, like a boom box or a loaf of bread. What is your reaction to someone who persists in a request like the neighbor does in the Gospel story? When is such persistence praiseworthy? When is it merely annoying?

Recall a silly gift you've received unexpectedly. Perhaps it was a Kewpie doll won at the county fair, a church bingo prize of a cookie cutter, a grab-bag gift of a rubber duck. Ponder the humor and sense of companionship the silly gift aroused. Or think of an unexpected gift from someone who you did not know admired you or who felt grateful for a simple kindness. Did the incident lead to a new or deepened relationship? Could unexpected gifts be merely a camouflage for the broader gifts of perseverance in friendship, kindness, or service?

Prayer. God of the universe, you created us to enjoy life while we prepare for happiness in the life to come. Help us today and every day of our life to find laughter and friendship in the unexpected gifts you give us.

PART 2

Mystery

mystery. A religious truth that humans can know by revelation alone and cannot fully understand

The Attic

The attic of our old farmhouse was unfinished. In order to walk across it, you stepped on the planks. If you accidentally stepped between the planks, the plaster gave way, leaving your foot dangling through the ceiling of an upstairs bedroom.

The only access to the attic was through a trapdoor reached by using a tall stepladder. On rainy, cold days when there was nothing interesting to do outside, we farm kids retreated to the attic. To get through the trapdoor required dexterity. You climbed to the top step of the ladder, pushed the trapdoor open, grabbed both sides of the opening firmly, and then swung yourself to the floor above.

I couldn't do it. I was too little. So I stayed in the hall below while my siblings called out imaginative tales about what the attic contained. They would shower me with wood shavings and small pieces of plywood. Actually, that's all the attic contained. We had never used it for storage. But for me, stuck on the floor below and able to see only a section of the rafters, the attic remained a place of mystery, an exciting place I was unable to enter.

Later, when I grew older and mastered the attic entrance, I was disappointed with what I found. The mystery was gone forever.

Pause. Recall a place that held great mystery for you when you were a child.

Scripture

Read about Elijah's encounter with Yahweh, 1 Kings 19:9–15.
Then read the Transfiguration account, Matthew 17:1–8.

Reflection

Mystery plays an important role in everyone's life. Think of
the mystery of seasonal changes or of two people in love. The
danger is that mystery can become commonplace. The seasons change so gently that we hardly notice when it happens.
Relationships die and are replaced with new relationships.
In our daily round of duties, we lose track of small mysteries,
such as the child gazing upward in awe at an unreachable
attic.

Our life touches profound mysteries, too. Unlike Peter,
James, and John, we may never see the transfigured face
of Jesus on a mountain, but we have all experienced peak
moments when we felt the presence of God intensely. If we
have learned to listen in the silence or to experience the
small mysteries, we have met our Creator there, too.

Where have you encountered the mystery of God's
presence—in mighty winds, earthquakes, or fire? Or has the
mystery appeared in the gentle breeze whispering softly in
your ear?

Prayer.

Great God of power, present in the roaring of the sea, the
flash of lightning, the destructive power of fire,
help us to use our strengths wisely.
God of the spectacular, who appeared to Peter, James, and John
through a gloriously transfigured Christ,
help us to see more clearly the times when you appear to
us in glory.
God of small, daily mysteries,
be with us as we walk through life; keep us attentive to
the small rustling breeze of your presence.

The Rosetta Stone

Resting as it does on a low pedestal in the British Museum in London, you could easily miss it. The Rosetta stone is an irregularly shaped piece of black basalt with cryptic symbols chiseled on its flat surface. Indeed, the stone attracted little notice from the throngs of tourists that warm July day in 1971. They were more interested in the mummy exhibit, one of the more colorful artifacts of British imperialism in North Africa.

The Rosetta stone, I thought as I looked down on it, was the clue unlocking the mystery of the ancient Egyptian civilization and providing another link to the first humans who walked this earth. Discovered in 1799 by a soldier in Napoleon's army, the stone listed funerary rites in three languages: hieroglyphics, demotic characters (a cursive form of hieroglyphics), and Greek. The Jesuit scholar Jean-François Champollion used his understanding of Greek to decipher, for the first time, hieroglyphic writing.

Archaeologists used Champollion's translation to unlock the meaning of other hieroglyphic texts, among them inscriptions on funeral urns, scrolls of business transactions, and the Egyptian *Book of the Dead*. This book is a scroll describing belief in an afterlife and giving directions on how to prepare the dead for the journey into the hereafter.

Pause. Think of an object or custom that unlocks the unique character of your family history.

Scripture

Read about God's love, John 3:16–17.

Reflection

Unlike Egyptian hieroglyphics, the great truths of our faith are waiting to be revealed. No clue, no matter how intricate, can unlock them completely. Saint Paul told the Corinthians: "Now we see in a mirror, dimly, but then we will see face to face. Now I know only in part" (1 Corinthians 13:12). After all, who among us can understand the God of love who sent Jesus to redeem us and offer us eternal life? We stand in awe at the mystery of God's goodness to us.

Knowledge, like that opened up through the Rosetta stone, most often leads to more mystery. So, for instance, being able to read hieroglyphics led scholars to ask more questions about why the Egyptians believed as they did about death. Similarly, Christians strive to understand the Scriptures more thoroughly so that we can stand in more profound awe of the mysteries of God's love.

After all, where understanding leaves off, faith begins. So even though we need to study and read the Scriptures and plumb the wisdom of our tradition, ultimately we walk by faith in God's love as revealed in Christ Jesus.

Can you recall an event that seemed mysterious at the time, but which later became clear? Did it lead to other mysteries?

Describe a circumstance in which you sensed the great mystery of God. Ponder the experience, recalling every detail and the emotions you experienced. How can you be more attentive to the God manifest in the mysteries surrounding you each day?

Prayer. Pray a litany of thanks to God for the mysteries of divine love offered to you each day. For example, "For the unexpected kindness of Terry, I thank you gracious God. For . . ."

Sand Dollar

When I lived in North Carolina, the sisters who lived nearby gathered periodically for prayer, sharing, and recreation. We tried to meet near the ocean so that we could spend our leisure time at the beach.

One of the sisters in our group was an excellent swimmer. She had grown up near the beach in south Florida, where she swam daily. One day while we were out swimming, I asked her if she ever found sand dollars. "Of course," she said. "I can feel them under my toes when I stand up in the water. I feel one now." She quickly dove under, appearing seconds later with a sand dollar.

Sand dollars don't look like the ones in souvenir shops. They are living creatures. Around their circumference are tiny filaments waving in the air. The creatures are, well, sand-looking, the perfect color to elude a predator in the ocean. In order to be saleable, sand dollars are sterilized and bleached white. When the cleaning is complete, only the skeletons remain.

Pause. Remember some wondrous moment of revelation that you received from nature.

Scripture

Read of God's omniscient love, Psalm 139:1–14.

Reflection

Like the people in the Hebrew Scriptures, we and all creation have a covenant with God. We cannot escape the covenant, even if we try. "Where could I go to escape your spirit?" the psalmist asks:

If I flew to the point of sunrise—
or far across the sea—
your hand would still be guiding me.

(139:9–10)

Like the sand dollar, we may not always be aware of God's living presence and supporting love under an ocean of fears, worries, and doubts, or even pleasures, blessings, and joys. Sometimes we have to dive deep, past the superficial, to find the mysterious presence of God in our experience. The abiding presence of the loving God is a living reality, but it is ubiquitous like the sand dollar. If we take the time to look with wonder, we can encounter God's presence in the ordinary.

The sand dollar mutely proclaims the mystery of God through its simple beauty. Unlike the sand dollar, we humans have myriad ways of celebrating our bonds with God. We can sing to the God who created our inmost being. We can serve others in honor of the one who knit us together in our mother's womb.

Describe ways homely objects reflect the oneness of God and the unity of all creation. What other natural wonders lead you to encounters with the mystery of God's covenantal presence?

Prayer. Take a quiet walk today. If going outside is impossible, sit comfortably and look out a window. Repeatedly praise God with the words of the psalmist:

For all these mysteries—
for the wonder of myself,
for the wonder of your works—
I thank you.

(139:14)

Mountain Hideaway

Some friends own a chalet in the mountains not far from Salt Lake City. My friend Angela and I asked to use it on a hot summer weekend. The chalet resembles other vacation homes in the area, brightly colored and trim, yet with the forlorn appearance of a building lacking permanent residents.

When we approached the building, my farm instincts led me to note the absence of electrical grounding. Other equipment needed for permanent housing was missing too, such as heating facilities and garbage containers, so the lack of lightning rods seemed unimportant. The chalet was, after all, used only for vacations.

We arrived in the evening and began preparations for dinner. While food cooked on the stove, we found comfortable chairs in the living room where we could watch the mountains framed in the large picture window.

Angela and I hadn't seen each other in months, so we quickly became engrossed in conversation, not heeding the sudden change in the weather. A storm had blown up. Suddenly we heard a loud metallic growl outside the kitchen window, saw a brilliant light, and jumped with the crash of thunder.

Fortunately we were too frightened to leave our chairs in the living room. After the storm died down, we returned to the kitchen to find that lightning had entered through the window, struck the burner where the potatoes were boiling, and then escaped outside.

After the initial excitement, Angela and I sat and talked about our close call with death. Had either of us decided to stay in the kitchen to mind the dinner . . . or had we decided to watch the storm from the kitchen window . . . who knows what would have happened?

Pause. Have you ever had a close brush with death or disaster like this? If so, bring it to mind.

Scripture

Read about true wisdom, 1 Corinthians 2:6–9.

Reflection

Our lives are surrounded by mystery. Think of the mystery of our marvelous bodies: a hand with the ability to create intelligible scratches on paper; the delicate mechanism of the eye capable of recording the colorful world around us. More mysterious is the *why* of our remaining in existence when others, perhaps younger and healthier, meet sudden death.

These mysteries are nothing compared to the mystery of the God who has promised wonders that "no eye has seen, nor ear heard, / nor the human heart conceived" (1 Corinthians 2:9).

Recall and ponder an experience you consider to be beyond the mind of humans. It may have been a profound experience of God's presence, a close shave with tragedy, a momentary transfixion at the sight of a new moon, the joy of daffodils blowing in a March wind. What made the experience so mysterious?

What mysteries of your faith do you find most challenging—the presence of suffering and evil in God's universe? creation and the afterlife? God's infinite love of all creation? Spend some time just reflecting on the mystery.

Prayer. Gracious God, I have faith, but grant me greater faith so that I can declare with my whole heart and soul:
Without any doubt, the mystery of our religion is great:

> [Jesus] was revealed in flesh,
> vindicated in spirit,
> seen by angels,
> proclaimed among Gentiles,
> believed in throughout the world,
> taken up in glory.

(1 Timothy 3:16)

PART 3

Sorrow

sorrow. Deep distress and regret, as over the loss of something loved

Paul

Nora served as a secretary at the Diocesan Pastoral Center in Salt Lake City, Utah. Everyone who worked at the center witnessed her faith and courage in suffering. Her husband, a judge, died suddenly of a heart attack, leaving Nora the sole breadwinner for a family of seven children. It was a difficult time, yet the family stayed together. A source of happiness for Nora was the decision of her oldest son, Paul, to become a priest. He had talked with counselors, joined other seekers in a vocation retreat, and committed himself to entering the diocesan seminary the following year.

After making the decision, Paul decided to go on a camping trip in the mountains of southern Utah. The mountains are rugged, spectacular, and crisscrossed with plenty of hiking trails. Paul and two friends settled on spending the weekend at one of the most picturesque places: Dead Horse Point. They assembled tents and hiking gear and left for the camping area. The next day, while they were hiking, a sudden storm blew up. The Utah mountains are famous for their fierce storms, lightning, and hail. Caught in the midst of the storm, the three men huddled together out on the open plateau. Suddenly a bolt of lightning struck the group, sparing the two friends but killing Paul instantly.

In a brief space of time, Nora had to cope with the deaths of both her husband and oldest son.

Pause. Bring to mind and heart a loved one or close friend of yours who died suddenly.

Scripture

Read about God's promise in Isaiah 49:13–15.

Reflection

Death is always a mystery, especially the death of a young person who we presumed had many years left to enjoy life and to grow in faith. We puzzle over how a just God could allow this to happen to a widow so soon after her husband's death. That Paul was killed and not the other two young men added to the sense that his death was willed and not just a random act of nature. The more we agonize over the mystery of Paul's death, the more we face our helplessness and our need for solace. People have always tried to make sense of suffering, as if we could reason our way out of sorrow. Why Paul? His death made everyone face those ageless questions that we ask in the midst of our sorrow.

Lest we blame God for our sorrow, Isaiah reminds us that God abides with us always and will never abandon us. So if God is with us at all times, God certainly is with us in our sorrow, too. God weeps with us.

Why is it so hard to accept the mystery of sudden, unexpected death—or, for that matter, expected death? Why is it tempting either to blame God or to rationalize that God wanted Paul, for instance, to be in heaven, and so took him? Do blame or reasoning really help us in our grieving? Invite God into conversation about your sorrow over the loss of a beloved person.

Prayer. Remember young people who died, as we perceive it, before their time. Include the following:
- Nora's son Paul
- family members and friends who died when they were young
- the Holy Innocents
- Stephen, the first deacon
- the children who died of starvation because of tribal conflict in Africa
- children of the Holocaust
- victims of child abuse

Bless these children and young adults, and ask them to pray for you.

Pray for God's peace for the families and friends they left behind.

Springbank

The happiest and saddest moments of our life are often associated with places—the home we lived in as children, the church we attended while young, the cemetery where our loved ones lie at rest. Retreat centers can be like that, too. Springbank Retreat Center in Kingstree, South Carolina, is one of those places dear to me.

During my frequent visits there in the 1970s, the property—a former plantation—belonged to the Dominican priests of the Southern Province. The white pillared mansion is a restored version of the original, which was destroyed by fire many years ago. Magnificent oaks and magnolias, their branches dripping with Spanish moss, grace the spacious grounds.

The people who lived at Springbank made it a center of welcoming and refreshment. The retreat director, John Egan, OP, encouraged a Catholic Worker brand of hospitality. Friends and passing strangers felt free to join the extended family around the table for the evening meal. The food was simple but nourishing, usually served late in the evening after the community shared in its preparation.

In the early morning hours before the celebration of the Eucharist, John would take his breviary, climb atop an old slide in the yard, and say his Office while reflecting on the sunrise.

The simple sharing of the Springbank community attracted many people seeking a time apart to reorder their lives. Attracted too were poor, rejected, and despairing people. They drank deep of the wordless comfort and support the community offered.

After leaving the South, I found other retreat centers to replace Springbank, but the memory of that place stayed with me. It was at another retreat center, Maggie Valley, that I learned of John's death. He had died two weeks earlier of a massive heart attack.

At the memorial Mass, people of every skin color, class, and lifestyle crowded the Springbank chapel. Through them the Spirit proclaimed the fruits of simple living in Jesus' name. Mourners remembered John's *pre-dieu* and climbed the tottering old slide to sit in the place where one they loved had spent so many hours in prayer.

Pause. Recall a place that has become a source of peace and refreshment for you, especially in your sorrow.

Scripture

Read Psalm 23.

Reflection

The Gospel is taught best by living it. The Springbank community, by sharing its home and meals, its prayer and silence, recreated a community of Jesus and his followers. Long before the word *inclusive* became popular, the community opened its home to everyone, freely sharing what it had.

Then John, who gifted the community in so many ways, stepped into the next life, leaving the rest of the community. Yet in the words of Bede Jarrett, OP, the gift remains:

Not as the world gives do You give,
O lover of souls.

What You give, You do not take away,
for what is Yours is ours also if we are Yours.

John found his gift returned by God's hand guiding him through the psalmist's "dark valley" and into the bright light of eternity.

Recall recent deaths in your family or among your friends. What places do you associate with these deaths? Recall other places that form a part of your identity and add stability to your life. Describe how these places help you to face death.

How can a community of believers give comfort to those who mourn? Think of examples from your own life, and give thanks to God for them.

Prayer. Slowly read and reflect on the following passage from Bede Jarrett, and then pray Psalm 23.

And life is eternal and love is immortal,
and death is only a horizon
and a horizon is nothing but the limit of our sight.

Lift us up, strong Son of God;
that we may see further;
cleanse our eyes that we may see more clearly;
draw us closer to Yourself
that we may know ourselves to be nearer
to our loved ones who are with You.

A Mother's Love

A mother's love has a special quality. Jesus referred to this special love when he mourned over Jerusalem. "How often have I desired to gather your children together as a hen gathers her brood under her wings" (Luke 13:34–35).

My friend Bert had a mother with a limitless capacity for love, but he didn't realize it until he was ready to die. He was a gay man, proud of his sexual orientation. He recalled walking the streets of Washington, D.C., his dress and stride proudly proclaiming his gayness. He was a good and kind person who helped neighbors in need. At a time when I was ill but needed to move immediately because of an expired lease, Bert and his friend Michael stepped in and moved all my possessions, then took me into their home to recover.

Bert had reluctantly agreed to an open relationship with his lover. It wasn't long before Bert contracted HIV. He continued working as long as possible. Then, as his strength ebbed due to AIDS, he quit his job and went home to die.

I heard about Bert's death after I sent a Christmas card to his home in North Carolina. His mother wrote in response, telling how she, her husband, and children had welcomed Bert with open arms. The family took turns nursing him until his death. After Bert died, his mother said, she applied bright-red lipstick to her lips, then planted a sloppy kiss on her son's cold forehead. "I wanted him to take my love with him into eternity," she said simply.

Pause. Bring to heart and mind someone you know who is dying of AIDS, cancer, or some other terminal disease.

Scripture

Read of Mary's vigil beneath the cross, John 19:25–27.

Reflection

Simple, accepting, nonjudgmental love leads us to be faithful in hard times as well as in sunny days. Washing sick bodies and cleaning up after vomit or loose bowels is far different from the romanticized version of love we see on television or at the movies. True love endures through all the vicissitudes of life—from the spitting, burping baby to the old person suffering from Alzheimer's disease or from a stroke that leaves the body broken and helpless. I received such loving kindness from Bert and Michael, and Bert received it from his family and friends.

Mary standing beneath the cross has become the symbol of suffering love. Her love didn't end with death. In the *Pietà*, Michelangelo captured Mary's sorrow as she held the dead Christ in her arms. Sometimes compassion, *suffering with*, is all we and even Mary have to give.

Imagine yourself with Mary as she watched her son die. What must she have been going through? Reflect on a time when all you could do was suffer with a beloved. What strengths were distilled in the fire of suffering love?

Prayer. Ask God for the strength that true love confers and demands. Try to be particular in your requests. Then commend yourself and all people to the compassion of Mary.

A Time for Healing

Maggie Valley is an ideal place for a retreat. At every season, nature displays her finest dress, and the retreat center, located in the Great Smokies, offers a spectacular view of the surrounding hills and valleys.

I chose to make an early spring walking retreat when the trails were still blanketed with last year's leaves, and only a faint hint of spring could be detected in swelling buds and the call of birds returning from the South.

The retreat, conducted by a Mexican priest named Ramon and a married couple, took us each day into a different area of the Smokies. We packed lunches, dressed in our most comfortable hiking gear, and went by car to the place where the trail began. It's easy to get lost in the mountains, so we were instructed to keep in contact with one another and to meet at a specific location for Mass and lunch.

Early in the retreat, tensions developed between Ramon and the couple on the retreat team. They had been chosen, it became clear, because the husband had Indian ancestry. He enriched our walks with tales of Indian lore. When we returned to the retreat house in the afternoon, he directed us in woodworking and other crafts. The wife appeared to be the spokesperson for the two. She liked to talk and was aggrieved when Ramon cut her off in the middle of her monologs. The tension drifted to the retreatants, temporarily marring the peace and healing that came from our communing with nature.

In those silent walks, my own tensions came to the surface. My sister Thelma had died a year earlier. I thought the mourning was over, but I was wrong. It remained, spreading tension similar to the aura of discomfort wafting from the retreat team. Intellectually I had accepted my sister's death, but the emotional residue remained: anger, discouragement, a deep sense of loss.

It all came together at one of our retreat liturgies celebrated near a small, noisy stream. A large rock in the center of the stream became the altar, making it necessary for the celebrant and the eucharistic ministers to wade into the stream.

Ramon began his homily by telling about a dear friend who had died of AIDS. He spoke of the many deaths in our own life and the need to see these losses as stages of the journey into God's presence. He ended the homily by taking a leaf and dropping it into the water. As the current carried it away, he whispered, "Good-bye, Bill." I knew immediately that I had to float a leaf for my sister. Two retreatants helped me to the bank of the stream, and I set my leaf afloat with words of love and farewell to my beloved sister. Healing began afresh.

Pause. Is there some sorrow that you can and want to let go of now?

Scripture

Read about the seasons of life, Ecclesiastes 3:1–8.

Reflection

Sometimes it requires a symbolic gesture to move us to the next stage of our life. The beauty of the Smokies, the sound of water gurgling in the stream, and a leaf floating away all helped us to visualize a movement from a time of grief to a time of healing. Sensitive people help interpret these symbols for us. Ramon, despite his own problems, became a channel through which God's healing grace flowed.

Ecclesiastes tell us that there's "a time for every occupation under heaven" (3:1). Recall a time in your own life when you passed through a season of planting, dying, or healing. Ponder it. Go over it in your heart and mind. If possible, share this time with others. If you still need to let go and are ready to do so, perform some simple ritual of letting go in which you also pray for the persons involved and for the graces you need.

Prayer. Select the most meaningful times of your life as inspired by the list in Ecclesiastes. Reflect on those times and the people who became channels of God's grace for you. Pray for them, and ask God to help you become a channel of grace for others.

PART 4

Humor

humor. The mental faculty of discovering, expressing, or appreciating the ludicrous or absurdly incongruous

Multiple Pizzas

My friend Marion describes herself as bossy. I'd call her a
good leader. Her assertiveness led to an amusing incident
when we visited the Italian city of Orvieto. Five of us in the
tour group decided to have lunch together. We selected a
sidewalk cafe that offered a *plat du jour*—pasta, pizza, and
beer. Judging by the size of pizzas in the United States, we
chose to share one pizza. However, given that none of us
spoke Italian, we were not sure how to make our wants known
to the waiter. Marion took the bull by the proverbial horns,
telling us that she would order. All we had to do was sit and
wait for our pizza.

By pointing and waving one digit, Marion got the message
across. The waiter smiled his understanding and then crossed
the plaza to the food-preparation center. A few minutes later
he emerged with one pizza. It was a bit skinny. Nevertheless
we divided it into portions and began eating while the waiter
stood by looking puzzled. A few minutes later he reappeared
with two more pizzas, then two more! He thought we had
ordered one pizza apiece!

Fortunately, as we sat laughing and wondering what to
do with all this food, more people from the tour arrived to
share our bounty.

Pause. Reflect on a comical misunderstanding you've
experienced.

Scripture

Read the story of the loaves and fishes, Mark 6:30–44 or
8:1–10.

Reflection

Miscommunication can lead to laughter, frustration, or even
anger. When miscommunication happens, it's helpful to see
the incident from the other person's point of view. In the
story of the multiple pizzas, for example, the waiter expected
customers to choose only the one item posted on the menu.
He tried to understand what these strange Americans wanted.
At least he didn't bring five beers and five pastas, too.

Seeing the Scripture story through the eyes of the crowd
gives it a different perspective also. For example, the mother
of the boy who brought food: "I must have misjudged the size
of the lunch I packed." A picky eater: "I wish he'd brought
something besides bread and fish." A practical type: "I wonder who did all that fishing." Jesus: "Isn't it great? These people sharing their food really is a miracle."

Place yourself in that crowd. What would it be like?
How would you react? Do you think that Jesus had a good
laugh about the reactions of the crowd?

The word *humor* is rooted in Latin words for normally
functioning body fluids. How does having a sense of humor, a
sense of the surprising ironies in life, help us to maintain a
healthy perspective of reality, a healthy balance in the fluid-
ity of life?

Prayer. Jesus, you are with us in even the most mun-
dane affairs. Help us to see you not only in the great liturgical
celebrations of our church or in times of silent prayer but also
in humorous incidents that keep us somewhat off balance,
and in the sharing of laughter with our friends.

A Community of Eccentrics

Cleaning the refrigerator at Oakwood House opens a wide door into eccentricity. The six women who live at this residence bring with them the idiosyncrasies nurtured by disparate backgrounds and lifestyles. The fridge reflects these differences: skim milk and 2 percent, butter and margarine. Helen likes a certain kind of bagel; Sharon, Philadelphia cream cheese (not the low-fat variety); Pat, black olives, avocados, and chip dip; Annette, grapefruit juice and coffee in a cup resting precariously on the top shelf near my non-dairy creamer. Mary Pat keeps her film and batteries on the bottom shelf near the bagels. Even the cat is eccentric. He likes only three varieties of a particular kind of cat food; the opened can requires refrigeration.

We are a community of eccentrics. The secret of living together in harmony, we've discovered, is to keep things in perspective, to look beyond our individualisms, and to see the whole person beloved of God. Respect for each person's uniqueness leads us to avoid trying to change one another. If God loves us as we are, then can't we do the same?

At our house, differences have a way of blending together pleasingly around the dinner table and later at community prayer. Each takes her turn at cooking dinner, the good smells sending a homey aroma through the house. The round dinner table is a place to share events of the day and to retell jokes—providing we remember the punch lines! The closing ritual—washing dishes and tidying the kitchen—provides more time for sharing.

Communal prayer is another bridge connecting our differentness. We read the day's Scripture passage and discuss it, each from her own perspective. Our viewpoints are a many-sided prism through which to reflect on God's word.

Pause. Think of a time or place in your family, circle of friends, small community, or some other group where individual differences emerge—possibly producing humor.

Scripture

Read Paul's exhortation, Romans 12:3–13.

Reflection

We are social beings, called to live in a family, a neighborhood, communities of many different kinds. If we try to pull away from everyone and live in isolation, our outlook becomes distorted, our eccentricities exaggerated. Living with others has its dangers, too. It's easy to become fixated on differences rather than looking for commonalities. If we see one another through God's eyes, our differences merge together into a loving and concerned community.

Paul reminds us that we are part of the Body of Christ. Our differing gifts serve the common good when we respect and support one another. A sense of cheerfulness, attentiveness, prayer, and hospitality witnesses to our unity in Christ.

Think about the communities to which you belong. Do your communities reflect Paul's vision of the Body of Christ? What can you do to enhance the sense of community with these people? When do you simply have to let go, smile, and accept the humorous ironies of life with these people?

Prayer.

Trinitarian God, help us to see you in the diverse gifts we bring to our communities.

God of the ordinary, help us to see you in every event of our life.

Jesus, God's Son, you lived in community with your followers. Help us to live in the awareness that we are members of your Body.

Ask and You Shall Receive

In pre–Vatican II years, women religious were appointed to ministerial positions by their superiors. Rarely were individual sisters given a choice of ministry. One of my appointments during those years was to move from a poor school in Rockford, Illinois, to a larger, more prosperous one in the Chicago suburbs. The change was welcome: a more roomy convent and a smaller class size. We even had a cook!

Blanche, a young sister who arrived with me, was concerned that she might be sent to another school. The problem was class size. With a class of only thirteen students, Blanche feared that her superior would replace her with an older sister who needed a reduced teaching load.

Class size was no concern of mine. I had forty students, a large class even in those days. Yet, sympathetic to Blanche's needs, I agreed to join her in a storm of prayer for more students. God answers all prayers, and certainly this was a legitimate one, we reasoned.

The prayer blitz, or novena—half superstitious ritual and half prayer—consisted of reciting a brief formula prayer nine times a day for three days. If said devoutly, custom of the time had it, any request, no matter how far-fetched, would be granted. For three days, from Friday to Sunday, we recited the novena together. At the noon meal on Sunday, our local superior was called to the telephone. The congregational superior had called to announce a change. It wasn't Blanche who had the new assignment. It was I! I was to return to my former school. Blanche would inherit my class, thus having enough students to remain at the school.

Pause. Reflect on a time when your prayers were answered, but not in a way you expected.

Scripture

Read about effective prayer, Matthew 7:7–11.

Reflection

Sometimes we wonder if God really hears our prayers. At such times we need to call on reserves of faith and perseverance. God will answer us in due time. "For everyone who asks receives," Jesus assures us.

The answer to our prayers may not be what we expect. In my case it was a mystery why God sent me back to my former school. Perhaps I still had work to finish, and Blanche was needed at her new assignment.

Recall times when you thought that God had failed to answer your prayers. Did God simply give you an incongruous answer that you failed to understand?

What does the exhortation, "Pray always," mean to you? If you do pray for something, can you accept with humor the answer God gives?

Prayer. Make an act of faith in God, and vow to persevere in prayer. Then recite the Lord's Prayer (Matthew 6:9–13).

The Body Beautiful

Florence, Italy, with its many art treasures, is one of the delights of European travel. My favorite statue, Michelangelo's *David*, stands on a pedestal in its own gallery, where everyone has an unobstructed view of the sculpture. To avoid damage from camera flashes, the architects designed the gallery with available light sufficient for photos from every angle.

The perfection of the statue pleased me. A perfect body, from the strong, lean hips to the noble brow, it gave the impression of equal perfection of mind and spirit. I walked slowly around the statue, taking pictures from all angles.

Every tourist looks forward to showing snapshots of the trip and recreating the experience for the family. My photos were arranged according to the places we visited, so it took time to reach Florence, preceded as it was by Toulouse and Carcassonne in France, Bologna and Siena in Italy. When the pictures of *David* finally appeared, my brother-in-law Tony reacted instinctively. "He's naked!" he exclaimed. "The man's nekked!"

Tony has never lived down that outburst. Since that day, a photo of *David* mysteriously appears tucked away into every birthday and Christmas box he receives.

Pause. Recall a time when your spontaneous reaction surprised you and provided humor for others.

Scripture

Read the Song of Songs 1:1–4; 8:5–7.

Reflection

The Song of Songs is a canticle of love, not the platonic kind but full-blooded, body and soul, erotic love. Like the Song of Songs, David's statue is a tribute to the beauty of the human body.

We know that our body is beautiful because God created it. To believe that the spirit is more perfect than the body is a kind of dualism that degrades the physical side of our being. Yet this hatred of the flesh often unconsciously permeates our thinking, leading us to feel guilty about our own sensuality, which is one of God's gifts to us. Our senses add to life's rich texture: the robust taste of a red wine, the smell of bread baking, the sight of a giggling child, the sound of a flute, the touch of another body.

How do you celebrate your body? How do you take joy in it, even if it does not fit the current popular standards of beauty? Can you enjoy the physical pleasure of a good laugh?

Reflect on steps you can take to develop delight in your body and to foster a more respectful and lighthearted attitude toward sexual love.

Prayer. We are all beautiful in your eyes, creator God, despite the bags under our eyes, the cellulite on our thighs, the sparrow tracks that have become crows' feet. May we learn to see the humor in the culture's paragons of beauty. May we smile at ourselves in the mirror and celebrate the beauty of other people.

Jack the Cat(s)

Jack, an eighteen-pound, tan-striped cat, considers himself a full-fledged member of our house. He has his own chair in the living room, leaving it only when he sees an inviting lap on which to snuggle and purr.

Jack seldom strays far from our yard, unlike other cats in the vicinity. On one of my walks this spring, I noticed a sign on a telephone pole: LOST, a black-and-white cat with a striped tail; $50 reward. After returning from my walk, I told our household about the lost cat, then left for a weekend visit with friends.

The following Monday, Sharon, one of our house members, was in the kitchen preparing her breakfast when she heard mewing at the porch door. She opened it, expecting to find Jack, but saw instead a cat fitting the description posted on the telephone pole. The cat remained on the porch while Sharon consulted Patricia, another member of our household. Together they surveyed the animal and decided that, indeed, our porch held a fifty-dollar reward.

The owners of the cat, a telephone call quickly clarified, were a fifteen-year-old girl and her grandmother. They lived only a few blocks away, so it was a matter of minutes before they were at our door. When they saw the cat, both owners became teary-eyed, the young girl crying, "Oh, Jack, we're so glad you're safe!"

Our Jack met their Jack, we met our neighbors, and any thought of a reward vanished in the pleasure of our new acquaintances and in the stories we shared about cats named Jack.

Pause. Does a well-loved pet add pleasure to your life? If so, do you also have humorous tales to tell?

Scripture

Read the Creation story, Genesis 1:20–31.

Reflection

This story from Genesis seems to make humans masters of God's earthly creation. Perhaps stewards might be a better translation, implying as it does, care and concern. The reading makes clear that humans possess the seed-bearing fruit of trees and bushes, the foliage of plants, and animals. Not everyone agrees, however, on how animals should be treated. Attitudes vary from hunters intent on killing wild game to conservationists willing to do anything, even put their lives in jeopardy, to save endangered species. The medieval theologian Thomas Aquinas taught that "in the middle way lies perfection." In this case the middle way may consist in recognizing animals as God's creatures, as gifts to be cared for and respected.

Pets especially add delight and care to our life. All of us, whether we admit it or not, find calm and comfort in simply stroking a pet's fur. Mature, serious-minded adults gush on and on, telling stories of their pets' antics. What is your favorite humorous pet story? Recall it. Give thanks to God for it.

On the serious side, what are our obligations to creatures? As children we were taught that it is wrong to treat animals cruelly. Is it equally wrong to treat animals better than poor people who lack the basic necessities of life?

Prayer. God of the universe, you created and blessed the fish of the sea, the birds of heaven, and all living animals on earth. I praise and bless you for the marvels of your creation. Help me to show my gratitude by treating all creatures with respect, knowing that you love everything you created, no matter how lowly they may seem from a human perspective.

A Case of Mistaken Identity

A good belly laugh is the quickest way to puncture inflated egos. That's what happened one summer when nineteen college professors visited West Africa to study development policies. We had sleeping-car reservations for the train trip into Bamako, Mali, a communist country and one of the poorest on the continent. African time schedules and reservations don't work the way they do in this country. By the time we got on the train in rural Senegal, our reserved places had been taken by people who boarded earlier. After a great deal of wrangling in French, the local dialect, and a few English phrases, our guides accepted crowded accommodations for the thirty-hour journey into Bamako.

The trip was rugged. We survived, knowing that we had rooms in a spacious hotel in the center of Bamako. Our accommodations on the previous stop had been student dorms with lice-infested mattresses.

As we pulled into the Bamako station, we heard the songs of children, sounds of drums and flute, and lots of talk and laughter. What a pleasant surprise! Finally we were being treated with the respect we deserved. The city dignitaries were welcoming the learned professors from the West!

The ego trip didn't last long. The celebration, it turned out, was for dignitaries from the People's Republic of China. The communists had funded a hydroelectric plant on the Niger River; their representatives were being feted instead of us.

To add to our discomfort, we were bumped from our beautiful hotel to make room for the Chinese delegation. Our reservations were transferred to Le Motel, several miles from the city center.

Things turned out well in the end. The motel was adequate, even though the air conditioning was erratic and the plumbing didn't always work. On our long bus trips into the city, we gained perspective on the lives of ordinary people, one of our reasons for visiting Mali.

Pause. Recall a time when a pinprick of humor properly deflated your inflated ego.

Scripture

Read about choosing places at table, Luke 14:7–10.

Reflection

In this Scripture parable from Luke, Jesus reminds us to avoid taking the highest places at table. He understands our tendency to seek the best things for ourselves, even when we don't deserve them.

Unless we are firmly grounded in God's love as the source of our self-worth, our ego can be artificially puffed up by honors and titles. A healthy dose of reality can quickly deflate us. We have the choice of laughing at our false ego and embracing reality with gratitude, or choosing to be hurt, to withdraw and nurse our bruised ego.

Reflect on the difference between a real feeling of self-worth and an artificial one. What can you do to develop a sense of self-worth based on God's love for you? How can you celebrate humorous moments that help you to appreciate your dependence on God and the silliness of depending on having the best seat at the table?

Prayer. Sit comfortably in a quiet place. Relax. With a smile on your face, recall God's constant, loving presence. Keeping the smile on your face, pray repeatedly the phrase, "Those who humble themselves will be exalted." Hear God speaking through this passage. End the prayer with an expression of gratefulness for the gift of humor.

PART 5

Strangers

stranger. A person or thing that is unknown or
with whom one is unacquainted

Ethnic Rainbows

As a young woman in the early 1950s, my consciousness of racism was raised through the example of a strong woman. Sr. Esther LeZotte was one of those no-nonsense people who told the truth just as she saw it, speaking as plainly and openly to her religious superiors as she did to other sisters in the community. Esther and I taught together at a high school in Cleveland, Ohio, where the religious superior's autocratic ways were legendary. One of my freshman students was Sandra Clark, an excellent student who was biracial. At our first parent-teacher conference, I met both of Sandra's parents. The following year Esther selected Sandra to play the lead in the school's annual operatic production. Sandra was perfect for the part. She had an outstanding voice, a good stage presence, and a commitment to doing her best.

The selection of Sandra for the lead did not please Sister Andrew, the principal. She reasoned that the school's financial support might be endangered and its image tarnished if a black girl played the lead. Racism often hides behind economic insecurities and pseudoreputations.

Even Andrew, who was accustomed to instant obedience on the part of her subjects, was wary of approaching Esther, whose bluntness could be disconcerting. Nevertheless, Andrew approached Esther and asked the question, "Wouldn't it be better to offer the lead to a white girl, someone more representative of the community?" Esther got right to the point and snapped: "I'd give Sandra the lead even if she were purple. The girl can sing!"

Andrew and Esther have long since died, and I often wonder if they are seated together in heaven watching angels of every color singing praises before the throne of God.

Pause. Consider a time when you felt victimized because you were different.

Scripture

Read the story of Philip and the eunuch, Acts of the Apostles 8:26–40.

Reflection

One of the evils of stereotyping is its disregard for the individual by lumping together people of similar races, classes, or sexes. Paper-doll cutouts lack distinctive features. They can be ignored and rejected because they don't have feelings; they aren't like the rest of humanity. It's easy to close off our emotions when we see strangers in pain. They're different from us.

Esther treated everyone equally, without regard for color or class. Philip did the same, despite the fact that the man seeking conversion was an Ethiopian, a eunuch, a stranger. Skin color and other individual characteristics are part of our human nature. Far from detracting, they add to our humanity by providing a rainbow of colors that complement one another. All are called to God's love and to the Good News of Christ Jesus.

Can you think of one story from your life when meeting and accepting a stranger proved a blessing? Now look at your shadow: recall a story of a time when you blocked a stranger out of your life.

Prayer. Holy Mary, you were a young Jewish woman with the skin color and ethnicity of your ancestors. You would not recognize yourself in the pale pink and blue statues that our culture uses to make you more acceptable. Help us, your children, to love you in all your Jewishness and to imitate you by loving others just as they are—beautiful in their uniqueness and pleasing to God.

Finding Space

Metropolitan Community Churches is a gay fellowship reaching across the United States and into several foreign countries. I literally stumbled upon MCC in Raleigh while looking for a prayer group to supplement the liturgy in my parish. The first service I attended was in the minister and his lover's apartment. Realizing that I was late, I rushed up a flight of stairs and into the apartment, tripping over the couple's bed as I entered!

MCC's services tend to be on the charismatic side, with rousing hymns, personal testimonies, hugs, and handshakes. The only difference: the anguish in the voices of individuals describing their nonacceptance at home and at work, and the joy that a straight person would choose to pray with them.

Life was hard for that little group. They had managed to find a church willing to rent space for afternoon services. MCC was expanding, and it was no longer possible to fit everyone into the apartment. The joy at having found a satisfactory prayer space was short-lived. A few weeks later, the host church's minister called for a meeting with the pastor and board of MCC. At that painful meeting, the host pastor announced that MCC could no longer use the facility. The parishioners had decided that it was inappropriate for gay people to worship in their church. The meeting was brief. Once again MCC had no place in which to offer prayers to the God who made them and loves them.

Fortunately a United Church of Christ had no such inhibitions. They gladly sheltered MCC under their roof while the membership continued to grow. In time, MCC raised sufficient funds to purchase a church. Besides worship services, MCC uses the church for outreach and educational programs, thus adding to the diversity of religious services in the city.

Pause. Can we condemn people because of their sexual orientation—make them strangers—and still claim to be Christian?

Scripture

Read about the woman accused of adultery, John 8:1–11, and about judging other people, Matthew 7:1–5.

Reflection

It is easy to condemn people we don't know or don't understand, in short, any stranger. Our prejudices blind us to the many ways we resemble one another.

We are, after all, created from the same clay. When our prayers rise to God, they mingle with those from people of every age, race, and sexual orientation. God answers prayers, no matter how humans view the supplicants. To believe otherwise is to limit the compassion of God.

We know the two great commandments: love God and love our neighbor. In the Christian Scriptures, everyone is our neighbor. Did Jesus condemn the woman taken in adultery? Did he say, "Do not judge, and you will not be judged," or "Do not judge those who are like you, and you will not be judged"?

Prayer. Read Leigh Hunt's poem "Abou Ben Adhem." Reflect on and pray over the message it contains.

Abou Ben Adhem (may his tribe increase!)
Awoke one night from a deep dream of peace,
And saw within the moonlight in his room,
Making it rich and like a lily in bloom,
An angel writing in a book of gold.

Exceeding peace had made Ben Adhem bold;
And to the presence in the room he said,
"What writest thou?" The vision raised its head,
And, with a look made of all sweet accord,
Answered, "The names of those who love the Lord."

"And is mine one?" said Abou. "Nay, not so,"
Replied the angel. Abou spoke more low,
But cheerily still; and said, "I pray thee, then,
Write me as one who loves his fellow-men."

The angel wrote, and vanished. The next night
It came again, with a great wakening light,
And showed the names of those whom love of God had
      blessed;
And, lo! Ben Adhem's name led all the rest.

Inside Prison Walls

We're all imprisoned within ourselves, looking outward in hope and enthusiasm, or avoiding the outside through fear of hurt or rejection. Surprisingly, I found people willing to move outside their own prisons in a prison itself.

Keith was a model student in my world cultures class at Gus Harrison Regional Facility, a state prison for men, located on the outskirts of Adrian, Michigan. Keith was a leader. When volunteers were needed to give reports or to read for the class, he was the first to raise his hand.

The students in the predominantly black class were friendly and cooperative. They were grateful that anyone from the outside chose to teach at the prison. The class syllabus included a guest speaker on Japanese culture. Sister Magdalena, a tiny woman from Tokyo, agreed to give the lecture. We met together to discuss problems that might arise in a prison class. I needn't have bothered. Magdalena is a born teacher who attracts students by her openness and simplicity, her humor and wisdom.

What I wasn't ready for was my students' preparation. Keith had researched a few Japanese characters and taught them to the class. When Magdalena entered the classroom, the students rose, bowed, and greeted her with a reasonable facsimile of a Japanese welcome. They repeated their bows when the class ended. The students enjoyed the lecture and spoke often of Magdalena in later class sessions.

Student creativity didn't cease with the guest lecturer. Keith encouraged one of the younger students who showed promise as an artist to create thank-you notes for the prisoners to sign when the class ended.

Pause. Think of a time when you found people open to others and to new ideas in a place where you least expected it.

Scripture

Read the Last Judgment, Matthew 25:31–41.

Reflection

At the Last Judgment, Christ will place on his right those who helped poor, sick, and imprisoned people. In helping them, they served Christ. Like the elect, we may not realize when we've seen God's face in others: those in prison or imprisoned in their own fears and angers, for example.

We can choose to imprison ourselves by becoming victims of past painful experiences, or we can move beyond our feelings and begin anew. Our body may be in prison, but our mind and spirit can be free. My students at the correctional facility taught me that lesson over and over.

Are there any fears, worries, griefs, or possessions that imprison you or make you afraid of the stranger? Talk with Christ about how you might break your chains.

Prayer. At the Last Judgment, Jesus will place on his right those who helped others in need. Reflect on these needy people:

I was hungry . . .
I was thirsty . . .
I was a stranger . . .
I was naked . . .
I was sick . . .
I was in prison . . .

Ask Jesus for the grace to see him in everyone you meet, especially in the stranger.

Poverty Hidden

Poverty can cloak itself in respectability. Cast-off clothing, when worn with style, can give the illusion of prosperity. Hunger can hide behind an innate sense of courtesy that keeps a person from begging for food or stealing it, the hunger revealed only in pleading eyes. Perhaps that's why we tend to avoid eye contact with poor people.

A group of us experienced poverty firsthand when we visited the Shrine of Our Lady of Guadalupe in Mexico. Our guide had provided huge bag lunches, more than anyone could eat. When we protested, the guide advised us to give away any uneaten food.

The visit was inspiring. We pondered the faith of a people who gathered in such huge crowds to pray at the shrine. It was a very warm day, however, and we were eager to find a quiet spot where we could relax and eat our lunch. But crowds were everywhere, and the shrine's caretakers kept hurrying us along whenever we approached what we thought might be a suitable spot. We finally chose a wall beside a landing on one of the many steep stairs at the shrine. We perched on the wall and began eating our lunch.

As we were eating, an artist in our group noticed an old gentleman and a little girl sitting nearby. They were genteelly dressed, the old man wearing a hat and winter jacket, even though the sun was beating down on him. The little girl wore a long dress that hid her thin little body. They sat silently, their eyes glued to the food we so obviously were enjoying. Suddenly we became aware that here was physical hunger.

Our lunches were all but consumed; only cookies, potato chips, and a fruit drink remained. Shamefacedly, we offered these crumbs to the man and child, receiving a whispered "gracias" in return.

Pause. When do you encounter poor people? Are poor people strangers to you?

Scripture

Read about fasting, Isaiah 58:6–10.

Reflection

The fast that pleases God, Isaiah says, consists of sharing our goods with the poor and helping the oppressed. Poverty has many faces. Nevertheless, in every guise, it reflects the unjust distribution of the world's resources. The young and the old suffer the most when we allocate to ourselves the largest share of the earth's bounty.

Reflect on Isaiah's list of the qualities of fasting that God desires. Then ask yourself: How do I or can I loose the bonds of injustice? let the oppressed go free? share bread with the hungry? bring the homeless poor into my house? cover the naked? be open to my kin? let my light shine?

Prayer. Talk with God about the help you need to do the fasting that is pleasing. Thank God for the blessings you enjoy.

Concentric Circles

Donations to self-help agencies have a ripple effect. Like a stone dropped into the water, the concentric circles ripple farther and farther from the point of entry.

The ripple effect could be observed at a clinic on the outskirts of Mexico City. A Canadian dentist gives a yearly donation to the clinic. The remaining funds come from small donations and fees clients are able to pay for services.

When we arrived at the clinic on an April Monday, the director, Soledad, was taken aback. She had expected us the following day and was unprepared for the arrival of seven guests. We laughed together, and then Soledad assured us that, even though the clinic was closed on Mondays, we were welcome to visit and learn about the health programs geared especially to women and children.

We visited the dentist's office, staffed three days a week by a local dentist; the room where the staff learned to give massages; the pharmacy where other staff learned how to prepare herbal medicines; and, as we neared Soledad's office, of plans afoot to teach acupuncture skills.

As we sat and talked, Soledad described a catastrophe that had occurred the previous night in an area near the clinic. A fire had broken out, quickly consuming the makeshift shacks clinging to the steep hillside. A child had died in the blaze; the people were homeless, temporarily sheltered in a school gym. Soledad broke into tears when she described the destruction. The women at the clinic had begun collecting food and clothing, she said. They were planning to walk to the gym that afternoon to deliver their donations. When pressed as to the cause of the fire, Soledad said she suspected that landowners wanted the squatters off the property so that they could use it for commercial purposes.

After giving our donation, we left the clinic feeling certain that the circles of self-help would reach the destitute people whose homes had been destroyed. As we boarded the bus, we could see children going from door to door collecting donations for the victims.

Pause. Recall a time when your community responded quickly and compassionately after strangers suffered a major catastrophe.

Scripture

Read about the apparition at the oak of Mamre, Genesis 18:1–15.

Reflection

Abraham and Sarah offered hospitality to strangers, giving them the best calf in their flock, the finest flour in their bins. Yahweh, disguised as a stranger, responded to this generosity by answering the couple's unspoken needs. Sarah, despite her disbelieving laughter, would give birth to a child. The effect of their hospitality ripples down to us today. Every Christian and Jew is a spiritual daughter or son of Sarah and Abraham.

Soledad and the women of her clinic provided a like kind of hospitality. Human ingenuity is an amazing thing. Given a little hope and a few resources, people can devise programs to assist both themselves and those in worse circumstances. A sprinkling of humor and a great well of compassion add a heroic quality to human ingenuity.

Have you seen the ripple effects of your hospitality or service to strangers? Are there projects to help people improve their lives that invite your assistance? What graces do you need from God to grow in service? Ask God.

Prayer. Seat yourself comfortably. Remember the people in your life who taught you how to fend for yourself, who enabled you to develop your talents. Then think of the strangers who entered your life only briefly but who made a lasting impression on you. Pray that you, like Abraham, Sarah, and Soledad, may always welcome strangers to your door. Pray repeatedly: "By serving the poor, I am serving God."

And the Greatest of These

When you're homesick, both the body and spirit suffer. You long for familiar surroundings and home-cooked meals. My bout with homesickness occurred in London, where I found the food particularly unsavory. Everything seemed over-cooked or overboiled, piled on a plate in a great glob of un-appetizing gunk!

One place where you could order omelettes somewhat like those at home was a little restaurant just around the corner from the British Museum. The price was reasonable, but you had to arrive early in order to be seated. The restaurant was cramped, the tables squeezed together.

One day when I sat down for lunch at one of the small tables, I noticed a man seated at a table inches away from me. He had an unlit pipe in his mouth and was reading a newspaper.

When my omelette arrived, the man put down his newspaper and began speaking in fractured English. He was a jovial man, so when his German version of English was insufficiently clear, he resorted to pantomime. We laughed a lot. I explained that my home was in the United States, and I was finishing research on my dissertation in European history. Enthusiastically I explained that Karl Marx studied in the British Museum during his exile from Germany. I was curious to find what documentation the museum had on Marx.

My fellow stranger explained that he was a salesman, though despite his pantomimes and frequent explosions of laughter, I was never quite able to figure out what he sold.

When we parted, I told my new friend that I would like to visit Germany, but unfortunately I couldn't speak the language. "That's not a problem," he mimed raising three fingers of his hand. "You need only three words: *Ich liebe dich*," I love you.

Pause. Think of a time when you were lonesome or homesick and someone helped to lighten your heart and help you become a neighbor.

Scripture

Read about spiritual gifts, 1 Corinthians 13:1–13.

Reflection

"And now faith, hope, and love abide, these three; and the greatest of these is love" (1 Corinthians 13:13).

Ich liebe dich: I love you. Love is all God wants of us. That German salesman gave me a precious gift, a random act of blessed kindness. He was a moment of God's mercy and love, right there in that packed restaurant.

Granted, love isn't always so easy. Love can be a hard virtue that requires speaking the truth to those we love. If we really love others in Jesus' name, that can mean helping them to be independent, giving correction when needed, and always being ready to listen lovingly. In short, to love is to wish the very best for the beloved. Whether simply given or done with great sacrifice, love (God is love) saves us.

Recall times when you received simple acts of kindness from a stranger who immediately became a good neighbor, even if the moment was fleeting. Bring to your mind and heart occasions when you have acted kindly, making a stranger a neighbor.

Prayer. Thank God for the invitations to love that strangers give us, and for the kindness of strangers. Ask God to help you steadily and cheerfully open your gifts to strangers.

PART 6

Neighbors

neighbor. To associate in an amicable or friendly way

And Who Is My Neighbor?

When I lived in La Crosse, Wisconsin, a tragedy occurred at Viterbo College. One of the students, a media-radio communications major, was killed in a car accident. The grieving parents decided to establish a tuition scholarship in memory of their son. They wrote and asked for contributions from three media personalities whom their son had particularly admired. Two of the personalities sent autographed posters. Garrison Keillor of *Prairie Home Companion* did more: he volunteered to give a memorial performance at Viterbo College. The cast of the popular radio show was in the Twin Cities at the time. It was a short trip south along the meandering Mississippi and then across the bridge and into La Crosse.

The Viterbo community was delighted. The fifty-dollar seats were quickly snatched up. Extra space had to be created onstage for the overflow audience.

Keillor, in a white suit and contrasting red socks and tie, won everyone's heart. The jokes and stories were tailored to life in La Crosse. Keillor even managed an anecdote about the Franciscan Sisters who sponsor the college.

After the concert Keillor accompanied the mourning parents to the grave of their son.

Pause. Recall a moment when you were moved to tears by another person's sorrow.

Scripture

Read the story of Tobit and his dead kinsman, Tobit 2:1–8.

Reflection

Compassion is a marvelous virtue, reflecting as it does the mercy of God. Neither Keillor nor Tobit in the Scripture story knew personally the person he was mourning. Compassion for a stranger like Keillor's or Tobit's touches our heart deeply, for we know that no social pressures, no psychological needs, and no desire for publicity elicit the response. It flows from a single-minded desire to help someone in sorrow.

Unlike Tobit, we will probably never risk banishment for unlawfully burying a dead kinsman. Yet the opportunities to comfort the sorrowful are many. Like the Good Samaritan (Luke 10:29–37), Keillor recognized the sorrowing parents as his neighbors.

How many opportunities do you have to comfort the sorrowful through a sympathy card or by attending a wake or funeral? Have you shared a neighbor's small daily sorrows, like a promotion denied or a child's poor grades in school? What other opportunities invite you to share God's neighborly mercy?

Prayer.

For the strangers who will die today,
> we ask you, God, to send a compassionate neighbor to be at their side.

For the deceased of our own family,
> we ask your mercy, God.

For the gift of compassion, the ability to share in the suffering of others,
> we beseech you, God.

For openness of heart to accept the mercy of others in our time of need,
> God of compassion, we pray.

Nosy Neighbors

A telephone hung on the wall in our farmhouse kitchen. To call a neighbor, we turned the crank on the right side of the box, and it rang a number. Our number was a short and a long: a brief twist to the right followed by a longer one. The neighbors' numbers were variations of this system, like two shorts and a long or three longs and a short. The operator's office was in Wallingford, seven miles away. To call her— and it was always a woman—we rang one long.

Mother didn't let us use the phone very often. Everyone listened to the calls, she said. When we called a neighbor, we could hear folks picking up their receivers all along the party line. One of the worst offenders was Hannah, an old woman who seemed to have nothing else to do but listen to every call and then spread the gossip to the neighbors.

The winter before her death, my mother became very ill and had to be taken to the hospital in Estherville. It was the only hospital within thirteen miles of our home in rural Iowa. Late that night my father called from the hospital. He was trying to reach my brothers on a nearby farm. Mother would need a blood transfusion in the morning, and Dad was sure my two brothers had the right blood type. We were too worried about my mother at the time to notice the clicking on the line indicating that someone was listening to our conversation.

Early the next morning when my brothers arrived at the hospital for the transfusion, they were surprised to find a line of farmers ahead of them. Half the neighbors in the community had responded to the call for blood. Our nosy neighbor had listened to our conversation and then sent out a call for donors.

Mother survived the illness and gained a few more months of life, in part through the help of Hannah, our nosy neighbor.

Pause. Think about someone who seems hard to love and ask yourself: How can I discover good in him or her—the Christ-light in every human—and make him or her a neighbor?

Scripture

Read the story of Jesus and Zacchaeus, Luke 19:1–10.

Reflection

Sometimes the very people who rub us the wrong way become our greatest benefactors. Hannah alerted the community to our need, giving them the opportunity to provide help and support. Zacchaeus, though scorned by Jesus' followers, gave half his property to the poor, paid back those he had cheated, and seated Jesus at his table.

People who pester us are often trying to tell us, in their own way, of their deepest needs. They want to be respected, treated with dignity. Our feelings of frustration with another's peskiness may indicate our fear of involvement in a difficult relationship, our embarrassment that our friends might judge us for making unsuitable relationships, or our failure to love the "different" as Jesus did.

Who are some of the "nosy neighbors" and "tax collectors" in your life? Talk with Jesus about each one. In your conversation ask: What steps can I take to reach out to them? How can I be a good neighbor to them?

Prayer. God, you loved the world so much that you sent Jesus to show us how to live and how to treat our neighbor. Help us to love more selflessly by searching out forgotten and unloved people and by proclaiming through our life and actions that they, too, are part of God's holy community.

Lute

Our farm family fared relatively well during the Great Depression. The livestock and garden kept us supplied with food. The house, heated by a wood-burning furnace, was warm. Our clothes were worn, but clean and darned.

One of our neighbors, Lute Range, had needs he could not satisfy with his half-finished house and small garden plot. Everyone knew Lute. Kids met him on the way to school when they took shortcuts through his wooded land. Lute was a scary figure, especially to youngsters trying to steal muskmelons. Easily six-feet tall, with a bushy beard and scraggly hair, Lute looked menacing when he stepped from behind a tree as the unlucky child reached for a melon.

It didn't take long, however, to learn that Lute was a mild and peaceful man who fed the birds and wild animals. Squirrels became so tame they ate out of his hand. His garden was beautifully arranged, each bed built up with fresh soil and drainage channels on all four sides. Lute grew the biggest and tastiest tomatoes, corn, and potatoes in the community. He sold the vegetables he didn't eat to buy staples like coffee and sugar.

Lute seldom visited our house, knowing that we raised our own vegetables and, like the rest of our neighbors, were short on cash. When he showed up at our door one day with a bag of vegetables, my mother sensed immediately what had happened. Without cash to buy necessities, Lute was forced to live solely on his vegetables. Too proud to beg, he stood mute at our door, hoping someone would understand his needs.

Mother quickly accepted the vegetables, exclaiming about their size and beauty. Then, taking Lute's gunnysack, she filled it with home-cured sausage and portions of our slim supply of coffee, flour, and other staples.

Pause. Who are some "Lutes" in your community?

Scripture

Read the story of the boy convulsed by the evil spirit, Mark 9:20–29.

Reflection

Our obligations to our neighbor go beyond the necessities of life. We are called by Jesus to be sensitive to actions that affect our neighbor's feelings of dignity and self-worth. My mother understood that Lute needed help, but gave it without robbing him of his dignity. If we fail to empower and respect our neighbor, we invite the resentment that nurtures violence.

Our sense of dignity is diminished when we are patronized, treated as charity cases. My mother realized that Lute was an honest, productive man who had fallen on hard times. Rather than turn him away with empty hands while making excuses about our own poverty, she chose to respect Lute's dignity by paying him in kind for the vegetables we really didn't need.

The father of the possessed boy wavered in his belief that Jesus could actually cure his stricken son. Even so, Jesus did not humiliate him and send him away. Instead, in charity, Jesus accepted where the man was and invited him to seek a deeper faith; at the same time, Jesus cured the afflicted boy.

What charity do you do? Make an inventory, and then pray in response to these questions: Does my charity help others help themselves? Is it empowering charity, the kind that makes good neighbors?

Prayer. Find a quiet place in which to reflect on the art of graceful giving. Reflect on what you have received when you have given to your neighbor. Ask God to make you more alert to the hidden needs of others, and to help you choose the response that reflects respect and acknowledges that the giver also receives.

Jeb

My friend Evelyn and I invited one of our students to dinner one evening in Raleigh. We lived in campus housing on the grounds of Saint Augustine's College. Students at the predominantly black institution came from a variety of cultures in the Americas and Africa. The student we invited to dinner was a Baptist minister from South Carolina.

Jeb was late, but we thought nothing of it. We had learned that time was relative. When Jeb arrived, slightly flustered by his tardiness, we quickly served dinner and sat down to food and conversation. The discussion was lively, but Jeb appeared uninterested in the food. He merely picked at it. I wondered anxiously if we had prepared the wrong kind of dinner.

When we pressed Jeb to take a second helping, he refused graciously and then explained why he ate so little. "When you are invited to dinner, my momma always said, eat before you go. Then you won't be so hungry you'll shame yourself by eating like a pig!"

After the meal was finished and Jeb had left in a chorus of thank-yous, Evelyn and I ruefully surveyed the pile of leftovers. Our upbringing had trained us to believe that guests tend to show their appreciation by eating heartily and accepting second helpings.

Pause. What contrary cultural practices have you encountered?

Scripture

Read about the traditions of the Pharisees, Mark 7:1–13.

Reflection

Differing traditions do not detract from our humanness; they add to its richness. The difficulty arises when we cling to traditions that harm others, or when we use tradition as an excuse for not helping those in need.

When Jesus and his followers sat at table, they neglected the Jewish tradition of ritually washing their hands. Of course washing our hands is just good hygiene, but for the Pharisees it was a point of pride to follow the fine print of the Law and then lord it over everyone else who didn't. As always, Jesus catches the Pharisees by showing their hypocrisy; they use a loophole in the Law as an excuse not to support their elderly parents. Thus they stick to the letter of the Law, but miss the greater commandment of loving their neighbor.

Jeb followed his tradition by behaving in the gracious manner he learned from his mother. In a Southern culture where many African Americans suffered from hunger, curbing the appetite was a considerable sacrifice. As he ate lightly of our dinner, Jeb may have recalled times when "eating before you go" meant only the meager diet of the rural poor. But "eating before you go" also showed enormous sensitivity and kindness to hosts who were just as poor as you were. Evelyn and I marveled at Jeb's kindness and learned something new.

Jeb's adherence to tradition is just the opposite of the Pharisees' sticking to the letter of the Law. Jeb's tradition was meant to honor and respect other people. How do you extend hospitality to other people? Do you adhere to any customs that get in the way of the hospitality to which Jesus calls us?

Prayer. In conversation with Jesus, discern ways to become even more hospitable, especially to people who might be different from you. Close your reflection by thanking God for the gift of human diversity.

The Threshing Ring

In the Depression years, we had only one threshing machine in our community. Because the machine was so expensive, it was jointly owned by several farmers. By midsummer, farmers signed up if they wanted to be part of the "threshing ring." It was understood that every able-bodied man and his adult sons would be part of the threshing crew. They were needed to haul bundles of grain to the stationary machine and to pull the wagons of threshed grain to the storage bins. Threshing could be very dangerous. If a farmer lost his balance while pitching grain into the maw, he could fall into the thresher. Death would be swift and horrible.

Women and children were part of the ring. They gathered at the farm where crops were being threshed. The women prepared and served meals, usually in the yard under a tree. Children carried jugs of water to the threshers at break times.

When the threshers arrived at a farm, great excitement filled the air. The women baked dozens of pies and prepared typical farm dinners, the menu invariably including fried chicken and potato salad. When the men came in at noon, sweaty and covered with dust from the thresher, they ducked heads and arms into huge basins of water on benches outside, then dried themselves on roller towels, leaving behind stacks of soiled linen. Conversation was hearty, filled with jokes and laughter. The men teased one another and the servers. Wives joined in the banter, returning gibes with instant repartee.

The threshing ring moved swiftly from farm to farm, finishing at the home of one of the machine owners. There, after accounts were settled and each farmer paid the cost of labor and machine upkeep, the threshing ring ended with a community ice-cream social.

Pause. Recall a community project you shared with your neighbors.

Scripture

Read of everlasting peace, Isaiah 2:1–5.

Reflection

Threshing rings are now part of farm history, but something valuable was lost with their demise: people working together for a common goal. The friendly atmosphere of the ring left no time for petty angers and jealousies, grist for the mill of conflict. Survival just about depended on being neighborly.

We pray for the time prophesied by Isaiah when swords will be hammered into plowshares, productive tools for harvesting the earth's bounty. Our prayers must be followed by action. The threshing ring is an example of what group efforts can accomplish. Communities who work together for a common goal are the building blocks for world peace. When we share this peace-building effort, the words of Isaiah surely apply to us: "Come, let us go up to the mountain of the LORD, / to the house of the God of Jacob" (2:3).

An old adage says, "think globally, act locally." How can you act locally to make the world a more neighborly place, especially for needy neighbors? In a practical way, could you organize a modern equivalent of the threshing ring: a car pool? a snow-thrower ring? a communal garden? respite care for children?

Prayer. Ask God for the courage you need to be a peacemaker, a good neighbor.

True Friends

Mary Louise and Jane were close friends, bonding not through blood relationship but through common interests and values. They were as unalike as caviar and bullheads. Mary Louise, a brilliant college literature professor and French translator, wrote poems of exquisite beauty and always dressed tastefully. In sharp contrast, Jane preferred work clothes as she puttered around flower beds or emptied the garbage. She was a biologist and artist with a practical mind; she could fix anything.

Despite their differences, the two women were held together by an uncommon love that, though not exclusive, could be fiercely protective if either person was hurt in any way. Yet the relationship was one of equality, never of dependency. It is inevitable in our culture that their relationship aroused suspicion and raised eyebrows.

The earthly ties uniting Mary Louise and Jane shattered when Jane died of a lung disease. Mary Louise was never the same. She became distracted at work, often leaving her office to seek acquaintances who would listen while she told stories about Jane.

Then one day Mary Louise collapsed while shopping in a department store. She had suffered a stroke. The illness advanced by stages. For a few years she could walk with braces and crutches. She could speak a few words and was still able to attend the symphony and student performances at Siena Heights College, where she had taught for so many years.

As the illness closed in around her, Mary Louise was confined to a wheelchair and could no longer speak, read, or write. All that remained was the silence of her interior world. In this final period of waiting, she was sustained by Jesus' love as she had known it in the love of her friend Jane.

Death came quietly to this woman who had learned in life the meaning of love through the love of another.

Pause. Bring to your mind and heart a close friend who adds richness to your life.

Scripture

Read about Ruth and Naomi, Ruth 1:15–22.

Reflection

The Scriptures tell us of the close friendship between Jesus and the disciple John, who leaned on Jesus' breast at the Last Supper (John 13:23–26). Jonathan and David, and Ruth and Naomi also model the grandeur of friendship. Indeed, Ruth provides a wonderful description of what friendship means when she tells Naomi: "Where you go, I will go" (1:16).

We all need friends, people to whom we can expose our heart without fear of ridicule or betrayal. A good friend is better than all the gold of this world. When we find a friend, we cherish our relationship, no matter what gossips say. "Faithful friends are a sturdy shelter; / whoever finds one has found a treasure" (Ecclesiasticus 6:14).

Bring to mind each of your true friends: those who support and defend you, who nurture your life energy and mentor you. Hold them in your attention and reflect on your relationship. Then reflect on this question: What neighbors do I wish to bring into my circle of friends?

Prayer. In conversation, bring the name of each friend to God. Pray for each one, and ask God for the graces you need to be an even better friend.

Afterword

"Were not our hearts burning within us while he was talking to us on the road, while he was opening the Scriptures to us?" (Luke 24:32). Like the Apostles on the road to Emmaus, we long for someone to walk with us and interpret the Scriptures through our own life experiences.

If just one of the stories in this book of meditations has inspired you, made your heart burn within you, then its purpose has been fulfilled. The inspiration, one hopes, will lead you to go further and recall your own stories based on favorite Scripture passages. The meditations you have read barely skim the surface of the Scriptures. So many stories wait to be pictured through the lens of your own experience. Think of the prophets who fearlessly spoke the truth to their followers; the exquisitely crafted parables of Jesus; stories of strong women like Suzanna, Judith, and Mary of Magdala; the numerous angels who dot the pages of both the Hebrew Scriptures and Christian Testament.

How to get started? Here are some suggestions. Get a small, ruled notebook and a good pen. Bring these supplies and the Bible into your prayer space. Begin by praying for guidance. Then make two lists: one of your favorite Scripture readings, the other of stories you have found significant in your own life. The stories needn't be about major events; sometimes it's small, simple things that leave lasting impressions.

Remember: Preparing the two lists is the hardest part of writing the meditations. As you reflect on the two lists, connections will begin to form, and a pattern will emerge. Only then will you be ready to begin writing. After you've finished writing several meditations, it's time to begin using them.

Keep in mind, however, that preparing the meditations has been, in itself, a meditation. You may choose to use your meditations for personal prayer or for small-group prayer with family and friends. In either case, place the meditations on the coffee table alongside the Scriptures, where they can be read and reread, a reminder that the Scriptures are as immediate as our own life.

Luke tells us (24:30–32) that the Apostles, after they reached Emmaus, asked the stranger to stop and sup with them. It was only at the breaking of the bread, a familiar and homey family ritual, that the Apostles recognized Jesus. May you too find Jesus each time you break the bread of the Scriptures.